1

CREATIVE EDUCATION

NEW YORK RANGERS

MARK EVERSON

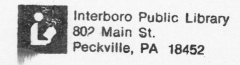

Published by Creative Education
123 South Broad Street, Mankato, Minnesota 56001
Creative Education is an imprint of The Creative Company

Designed by Rita Marshall
Cover Illustration by Rob Day

Photos by: Bettmann Archives, Bruce Bennett Studios, Focus on Sports,
Hockey Hall of Fame, Protography, Spectra Action, Sports Photo Masters
and Wide World Photos

Library of Congress Cataloging-in-Publication Data

Everson, Mark.
New York Rangers / Mark Everson.
p. cm. -- (NHL Today)
ISBN 0-88682-681-0

1. New York Rangers (Hockey team)--History--Juvenile literature.
[1. New York Rangers (Hockey team)--History. 2. Hockey--History.]
I. Title. II. Series.

GV848.N43E94   1995   93-48434
796.962'64'097471--dc20

3456

THE DREAM COMES TRUE

In the summer of 1994, New York City was bursting with enthusiasm and euphoria. The New York Rangers had won the Stanley Cup, and if they could do that, all things seemed possible.

For decades, Rangers fans had suffered the passing of the years without a championship. The taunts from their rivals grew, and a simple chant developed that embodied all the frustrations of these amazingly loyal fans. "1940" was all that was needed to be said to infuriate and silence Rangers followers. That quick squelch, and the source of all that pain, rested in one little sta-

Mike Richter celebrates the team's 1994 Stanley Cup victory.

tistic in the record book, which showed that in 1940, the Rangers won the Stanley Cup. It did not show them winning it again until June 14, 1994.

In those intervening 54 years, the team became something of a cult—supported not by those who expected instant success, but by those to whom waiting makes ultimate triumph more glorious. Parents who had never seen the Rangers win a Cup passed their devotion to their children. And despite the Rangers' failures, Madison Square Garden, in the heart of midtown Manhattan, was nearly always sold out.

Suddenly, all those years of waiting and hoping were repaid, and the outpouring of pent-up emotion and devotion was staggering. The fans finally had their chance to parade the Stanley Cup up Broadway. Lining the parade route were an astounding 1.5 million people—more than the population of some entire states. In some spots, the crowds were 30 people deep, all of them celebrating the day they had awaited all their lives.

The jinx has finally been broken, and now Rangers fans dream of more championships to repay all the years when they were deprived.

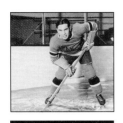

1 9 2 6

Frank Boucher led the team with 15 assists during their inaugural season.

TEX'S RANGERS

The Rangers weren't the first National Hockey League team in Madison Square Garden or even in New York. That distinction belongs to the New York Americans, born in 1925–26 with the bulk of a Hamilton, Ontario, team that was suspended for going on strike after winning the league's regular season in 1924–25. The owner of the Americans was "Big Bill" Dwyer, a Prohibition figure of the Roaring Twenties. There was only one problem: they didn't have a rink.

Sergei Zubov tallied 77 assists in 1994 (page 7).

Ching Johnson's tough, aggressive style led to his induction into the Hockey Hall of Fame.

That's where a remarkable man, George "Tex" Rickard, came in. Rickard was a fortune seeker. He'd been to the Klondike for gold, to South Africa for diamonds and to South America for cattle, and now he was back in New York to try his hand at entertainment promotion. He had just built the third Madison Square Garden in just eight months and needed attractions to fill the seats. Rickard and his associates thought hockey would go over big in New York, but since the NHL already had sold an expansion franchise to Dwyer, it was reluctant to grant another in the same area so quickly.

So the man who had a team but no rink got together with the man who had a rink but no team. Rickard allowed the New York Americans to play at the Garden in exchange for Dwyer's aid in obtaining a franchise for the Garden investors to own. That process took a year, and the Rangers were born May 15, 1927, when the franchise was granted to the Garden. The unnamed team quickly was dubbed "Tex's Rangers" in newspapers, and the name stuck. The Americans and the Rangers both played in the Garden until 1942.

Conn Smythe was hired to organize the new team and quickly assembled the nucleus of a powerful squad by signing brothers Bill and Bun Cook, Frank Boucher, Ching Johnson, Taffy Abel and Murray Murdoch. Bill Cook, Boucher and Johnson went on to become Hall-of-Famers with the Rangers.

Soon fired in a dispute with the owners over player acquisition, Smythe went on to buy the Toronto St. Patricks, rename them the Maple Leafs and build them into a league power. The NHL trophy for the most valuable player in the playoffs bears his name.

Smythe was replaced by Lester Patrick, who guided the Rangers as coach through the 1938–39 season and as general manager until 1946–47. Patrick, too, has a league trophy bearing his name, given to the outstanding performer as voted on by the players.

THE EARLY, GLORY YEARS

Manager Lester Patrick and coach Frank Boucher celebrated their second league championship.

Under Patrick, known as "the Silver Fox," the Rangers finished atop the American Division of the league in their first season, with Bill Cook winning the scoring title. They were ousted by the Boston Bruins in the playoffs that year, but the next year, 1928, they won their first Stanley Cup, beating the Montreal Maroons despite being unable to play a single game at home because the circus was in town. In that series Lester Patrick became a legend.

The Maroons already had won the opening game when a shot hit Rangers goalie Lorne Chabot in the eye, causing severe bleeding. Chabot was carried from the ice on a stretcher and never again tended the Rangers goal. Teams didn't have backup goalies in those days, and Patrick, the 44-year-old coach, was their sole option.

"Let 'em shoot," Patrick hollered at his defensemen.

"Don't let 'em shoot," screamed the Rangers from the bench.

Flopping and scrambling, Patrick allowed only one goal, and the Rangers triumphed 2-1, turning around the series en route to the Cup. Joe Miller took over in the Rangers goal for the rest of the series.

The Rangers went to the finals in 1929, falling to Boston, and again in 1932, losing to Smythe, Chabot and the Toronto Maple Leafs. In 1933 they won their second Cup, topping the Maple Leafs, but signs of age among the original Rangers began show-

John Vanbiesbrouck won the Vezina Trophy in 1986 (pages 10-11).

ing. They missed the playoffs for the first time in 1936. By 1940 the lineup had changed considerably. Patrick's sons, Lynn and Muzz, brothers Neil and Mac Colville, Alex Shibicky, Bryan Hextall Sr., Phil Watson, Babe Pratt and Art Coulter were now the big names, with Dave Kerr winning the Vezina Trophy as top goalie. Frank Boucher replaced Lester Patrick as coach and won the Cup in his first try—with Bryan Hextall's goal at 2:07 of overtime in Game 6 on April 13, 1940, bringing the Rangers their third Stanley Cup, and their last one until 1994.

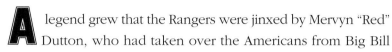

A LEGENDARY JINX

A legend grew that the Rangers were jinxed by Mervyn "Red" Dutton, who had taken over the Americans from Big Bill

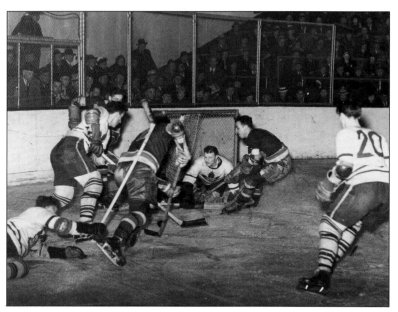

Dwyer. Madison Square Garden had declined to renew the Americans' lease, and they faded into oblivion, with Dutton later becoming league president. The tale became tradition, and one fact is certain: Between the time the Garden canceled the Americans' lease in 1942 and Red Dutton's death, the Rangers were unable to win the cup.

The Rangers managed to win the regular-season title in 1942, but were soon broken up by World War II, when the nucleus of the team joined the Armed Forces. The Rangers themselves nearly suspended operations during the war, winning only six of 50 games in 1943–44. They rose to return to the finals in 1950, behind the MVP goaltending of Chuck Rayner. Needing only to win one more game, they held two-goal leads in both Games 6 and 7, but lost both to Detroit.

The seventh game went into overtime, and Don "Bones" Raleigh hit the goalpost with a shot—the closest the Rangers would come for more than 40 years—before Detroit's Pete Babando scored the winner in the second overtime.

The Rangers would not return to the finals for 22 years, during which time there was a long succession of general managers, coaches and players. Andy Bathgate, Harry Howell, Gump Worsley and Camille Henry were the stars in a bleak sky, but despite their individual accomplishments, they were unable to bring home the Cup.

Fortunes turned and hopes began rising again when Emile Francis took over as general manager and coach, with Rod Gilbert, Jean Ratelle and Bob Nevin up front and Ed Giacomin in goal. Playing at the new Madison Square Garden at 33rd Street and Eighth Avenue, they won their first two playoff games in 1968 against the mighty Chicago Blackhawks. Dreams were beginning.

1 9 4 4

The team reached an all-time low, winning only six games all season.

Jean Ratelle won the NHL Lady Byng Trophy for his sportsmanship and playing ability.

"Bobby Hull [Chicago 50-goal scorer] came down with a charley horse," Gilbert recalled. "We were saying 'Great!' But Martin Luther King was assassinated and they postponed the game five days. That gave Hull time to get well."

In Game 3, Gilbert scored two goals six seconds apart, and it looked as though the Rangers had a lock on the series. But Chicago changed goalies and rallied to win that game, plus three more in a row.

ANNUAL DISAPPOINTMENTS

The talented Rangers remained a yearly preseason pick for the Cup, but never managed to fulfill the expectations. In 1970 the big, bad Boston Bruins ousted them with a rough-and-tough style. In 1971 the Rangers fell to Chicago in seven games, despite Pete Stemkowski's double-overtime winning goal in Game 6. In 1972 they made the finals for the first time in 22 years, but fell to the Bruins. In 1973 they dethroned the Bruins, but lost to Chicago.

The disappointments were becoming chronic. In 1974 they fell to the goaltending of Bernie Parent and the fists of the Philadelphia Flyers, and in 1975 their hated neighbors, the New York Islanders, knocked them out in the first round.

"That summer of '75, we got it from everybody," Pete Stemkowski said. "The postman wouldn't deliver the mail; he left it on the sidewalk. That was the beginning for the Islanders and the beginning of the end for us."

The Rangers were now owned by Gulf + Western, later Paramount, and began a period of constant upheaval as the executives sought to hire their way to a Cup. Emile Francis was fired

Tony Granato is an Extra Effort Award winner (page 15).

after trading Jean Ratelle and Brad Park for Phil Esposito and Carol Vadnais. John Ferguson, from the Montreal Canadiens, lasted two years as general manager before Fred Shero took over as both general manager and coach. Shero, a mysterious man who could quote Zen philosophy, had guided the Philadelphia Flyers to the Stanley Cup in 1974 and 1975 by employing a brawling, rough-house style. In 1978–79 he coached the Rangers to the finals against the Montreal Canadiens.

The fans held their breath.

REACHING FOR GLORY

That 1979 charge to the finals and its aftermath seemed to typify what Rangers fans endured. Tickets were selling for $500 each, an unheard-of sum then. For a month, everything that

Phil Esposito is the NHL's fourth all-time point scorer.

defines life in the Big Apple—the Yankees, Mets, Giants, Jets, Knicks, Nets, Islanders, the Metropolitan Opera, Broadway theaters, high fashion and even Wall Street—took a back seat to what was transpiring on the ice at Madison Square Garden.

Spring was in the air and the New York Rangers were front-page news, inspiring dreams among their fans and rekindling the excitement that THIS might finally be the year they would win the Stanley Cup. Rangers fans still were getting over the ultimate failure of their great teams of the 1960s and early 1970s. This Cup charge came without warning, and that was part of its lure.

They had only been back to the playoffs for one year after missing two straight seasons. They were still supposed to be rebuilding. It was their rival neighbors, the New York Islanders, who had won the regular-season championship and seemed poised to make their bid for the Stanley Cup.

After a sweep of the Los Angeles Kings in the first round, the Rangers advanced to meet the Philadelphia Flyers, the team Shero had quit for the Rangers less than a year earlier. The Rangers dropped the opener, then roared back to move into the semifinals—a renewal of the Battle of New York against the Islanders. It was the first time the rivals had met since the Islanders shocked the hockey world by ousting them in 1975.

"When we won against Los Angeles, nobody really noticed," recalled Rangers goalie John Davidson, the biggest hero of the run. "But when we got it going against the Flyers, that's when the fans started getting into it. Then we faced the Islanders and every game was a war, a flat-out war. Just great hockey. There was so much emotion on each side."

The teams split the first four games, then Davidson made one-goal leads hold up in Games 5 and 6, and the Rangers went to the Stanley Cup finals for only the third time in 39 years. The victory filled the front page of the New York newspapers and captured the imagination of the city.

Yet bad luck—or "the jinx," as some believed—was beginning to play its part. Davidson's knee was injured against the Islanders and would not hold up.

Meanwhile, the Montreal Canadiens edged the Boston Bruins in overtime of the seventh game of their series—a game that will be remembered as the night a Bruins game vanished in the final moments because Boston was penalized for having too many men on the ice.

"Fate had its way," Davidson said. "We were all watching that final game between Boston and Montreal. And I'm convinced we would have beaten Boston."

The Canadiens were a mighty team, winners of three straight Stanley Cups. Yet Davidson still had enough to limit them to one

1 9 8 1

Don Maloney set a Rangers' record for most shorthanded goals in a season with five.

Mike Rogers was the top point scorer for two years.

goal as the Rangers hit their high-water mark by taking the opener. The Rangers even had prompted the Montreal coach to replace Ken Dryden, the four-time All-Star goalie, with Michel Larocque.

Everything seemed to point towards the Rangers' first Stanley Cup since 1940 as the teams warmed up for the second game. Suddenly, an innocent practice shot from a teammate caught Larocque in the eye, and Dryden was pressed back into service. Given a second chance, Dryden wouldn't allow one to the Rangers. The Canadiens took over and won four straight games, ending the Rangers' bid for glory. They wouldn't return to the finals for another 15 years.

John Vanbiesbrouck was voted Rookie of the Year by the Rangers' fan club.

GETTING IT RUBBED IN

That heartbreak for Rangers fans was compounded over the next few years. The New York Islanders, the suburban team without the bankroll of the high-profile Rangers, rebounded from their 1979 loss to win the Stanley Cup in 1980. The Islanders went on to win the Cup again in 1981, 1982 and 1983. The Rangers became the second-fiddle team of New York.

Those were hard years for the Rangers and their fans, as the upstart Islanders and their backers began reminding the Manhattan team just how long it had been, chanting, "1940! 1940! 1940!"

As the Islanders began their Stanley Cup streak, Shero was replaced by Herb Brooks as coach and Craig Patrick as general manager. Brooks had captured the imagination of the United States by guiding the 1980 U.S. Olympic team to the gold medal. But he couldn't recreate that magic with the Rangers, and by 1985, Brooks had been fired.

Left to right: Darren Turcotte, Jan Erixon, John Ogrodnick, Brian Leetch.

Ted Sator became coach for 1985–86 and turned the team upside-down, sending stars such as Pierre Larouche to the minors. Larouche returned in time to help the Rangers reach the semi-finals, but that wasn't enough to save Craig Patrick's job. Phil Esposito became general manager and made more than 50 trades in his three years before he was replaced by Neil Smith in 1988.

Smith continued the Rangers' tradition of trading for star centers, first acquiring Bernie Nicholls from Los Angeles, then sending Nicholls to Edmonton for superstar Mark Messier, whose arrival in 1991–92 led to the Rangers' first overall regular-season championship since 1941–42. But that season of hope fell apart, too, as the Rangers fell to the Pittsburgh Penguins in the second round of the playoffs.

1 9 8 8

James Patrick played hard-nosed defense, adding 45 assists for his second consecutive season.

The next season, 1992–93, was a disaster, as the Rangers missed the playoffs, finishing last in the Patrick Division amid injuries to Messier and star defenseman Brian Leetch.

The morning after the final game, Mike Keenan was signed to the most lucrative coaching contract in league history. Keenan, who had been to the finals three times with the Philadelphia Flyers and Chicago Blackhawks, had the fans hoping again that, finally, an end would come to the decades of disappointment and waiting.

Keenan brought with him a reputation as a winner. Known as "Iron Mike" for his no-nonsense style of coaching and his demands on his players, Keenan orchestrated several quick player moves, notably adding high-scoring winger Steve Larmer, whom he had coached in Chicago. Even if a superstar made a mistake on the ice, he was liable to be benched by Keenan, who immediately made the point that errors would not be tolerated from anyone. His style of play relied on swarming pursuit of the puck

Adam Graves (#9) earned his first Steven McDonald "Extra Effort" Award.

and hard-nosed pressure on offense. The five-year contract Keenan signed, worth nearly $1 million a season, was quick proof that the owners were committed to him and his serious style, and committed to bringing the elusive Stanley Cup to New York, regardless of the cost.

THE ULTIMATE GLORY

As the 1993–94 season opened, the Rangers struggled, then caught fire at the end of October. They went 14 games without losing, taking over first place in their division and then in the league. They wound up with 52 victories, a franchise record, capturing the Presidents' Trophy as regular-season champs for the second time in three years.

Hopes had been built again, and a masterful sweep of the rival Islanders fueled them. A five-game triumph over the Washington Capitals, who had beaten them in their previous two meetings, raised the frenzy to fever pitch as they prepared to battle the New Jersey Devils, rivals who played only eight miles away and who had finished second in the league to the Rangers.

That series proved a classic, testing every ounce of faith Rangers fans had left. The Devils captured the opener after erasing a Rangers lead with 43 seconds remaining, and winning in dramatic double overtime. The Rangers then won two straight, taking the series lead with a double-overtime victory of their own. But the Devils rebounded to win two straight, putting the Rangers on the brink of elimination.

Undaunted, captain Mark Messier promised the fans victory in Game 6, then delivered by scoring three straight goals in the third

Steve Larmer played his first game as a Ranger on November 3, tallying the game-winning goal.

Tony Amonte added scoring power to the Rangers.

Mark Messier ranks tenth in scoring in the NHL.

1 9 9 5

The Rangers are counting on players like Alexei Kovalev, who had a stellar rookie season in 1993-94.

period for comeback survival. That extraordinary effort set up Game 7, one of the greatest dramas in franchise history. The Rangers nursed a 1-0 lead into the final moments, only to be tied with just 7.7 seconds remaining. The dreams moved into excruciating overtime, and then into double overtime, with the next goal propelling one team into the Stanley Cup finals, the other into summer.

Stephane Matteau, who had been the double-overtime hero in Game 3, came from behind the net to wrap in the goal that shot the Rangers into the Stanley Cup finals.

Next, the Rangers had to beat the Vancouver Canucks, and it would not be easy. The Canucks gave the Rangers another opening-game shock, triumphing in overtime. The Rangers then ran off three straight triumphs, putting them on the brink of ecstasy. The New York papers proclaimed "Tonight's the Night" for Game 5 at Madison Square Garden, but the Canucks would not cooperate. They won Game 5, then captured Game 6 in Vancouver, forcing a deciding classic in New York. As fearful as they were hopeful, the Garden fans still roared their support for the Rangers, who took a 2-0 lead and held on for a 3-2 victory, setting off a city-wide party that lasted for days.

The Rangers carried the Stanley Cup to Yankee Stadium, to hospitals, clubs and restaurants. There was no telling where it would show up next. It was a summer of celebration, after so many of disappointment.

Along the parade route, one youngster held a sign toward the floats carrying the Rangers. It read: "My grandfather thanks you. My father thanks you. I thank you."

Now that the jinx has been broken, Rangers fans are hoping for another long streak in the record books—this time consisting of Stanley Cup victories.